Poetry in Place
Autumn Writing from the Bosque

Albuquerque poets at the Open Space Visitor Center

Poetry in Place
Autumn Writing from the Bosque

Albuquerque poets at the Open Space Visitor Center
September 26, 2015

Edited by Jules Nyquist
Poetry Playhouse Publications
Jules' Poetry Playhouse, LLC
Copyright 2016
All rights revert to the authors

Table of Contents

Introduction

On Saturday, September 26th, a dozen or so poets gathered at the Open Space Visitor Center in Albuquerque, New Mexico. Ten of those poets submitted poems for this book on Autumn in the Bosque. Jules Nyquist, instructor, led a free writing workshop followed by a reading for anyone who wanted to attend.   Writers walked through the Open Space gardens and grounds. This event also concluded the gallery show "Bosque" where local artists interpreted the Bosque through paint, pastel and photography to serve as muse.

The Bosque, or forest, derives its name from the Spanish word for woodlands and has been a companion of the Rio Grande, expanding or shrinking depending on the whims of the water flow. The Bosque offers sanctuary to wildlife and more recently, people. It also offers inspiration.

In these poems, poets worked on cultivating their senses and capturing them in words on the page. Four of the poets are members of Crosstown Poets (Joanne Bodin, Jules Nyquist, Andi Penner and Susan Paquet) who led the group in writing and reading their work.   Photos in this book correspond with views from the Open Space and in Albuquerque.

Jules Nyquist is a poet and leads creative writing classes. She is the founder of Jules' Poetry Playhouse, LLC, an organization dedicated for poets writing and sharing their work. Her website is www.julesnyquist.com.

The Open Space Visitor Center is an interpretive hub for the Open Space program, lands, and resources. Visitors enjoy educational exhibits, art displays, wildlife fields, a Traditions garden, Bosque trails, and a variety of talks, workshops, demonstrations and entertainment.

The **Open Space Visitor Center** is located at 6500 Coors Boulevard, between Montaño Road and Paseo del Norte at the end of Bosque Meadows Road in Albuquerque, New Mexico. Look for the Flyway art installation. The website is www.cabq.gov/parksandrecreation/open-space/open-space-visitor-center

Joanne S. Bodin

Impermanence

clinging to your smooth wooden surface
carved by an artist's hands
into a statuesque obelisk formed from gnarled wood
Bosque wildlife spiral around you in wooden formations
reminding us that we grace their land in impermanence
you hold dear the frog, beaver, rabbit, roadrunner, possum,
snake
and on top, the proud and stately crane
beak pointing north
reminding us of early migrations

perhaps the artist who carved you knew about
seasonal change and impermanence
perhaps the nearby arroyo washed away his young son
one stormy New Mexico winter
or perhaps the cottonwood tree that you are
was found abandoned after fifty years
when someone finally noticed you
deciding to immortalize your trunk
by carving iconic imagery
or perhaps your roots never waivered
and you were the lucky one
captured by the eye of an artist

now, children run in grassy fields that surround
your statuesque presence
slide their fingers along your smooth surface
touch the fibers of your soul
as you continue to stand tall
for generations to come

Teresa E. Gallion

Fall Approaches

Fall walks slowly into the Bosque.
Sunflowers flirt with anticipation,
a prelude to the color fest.
Apples fall on the end of September,
lay quiet on the ground, a nutritious
donation to birds and other little critters.
Seeds reunite with the high desert sand.
My boots make music on the sidewalk.

Fall preparations
Yellow fire lights Bosque trails
Prepares winter's bed.

Ginny Gaskill

The Leaf Quakes

A leaf from the Aspen
wakes to its soft green.

Tiny, it put energy to growing.
Fully formed it glories
to the touch of the wind.
They call it quaking.

For six months it watches.
See bucks strut and fawns stretch
on spindly legs
reaching for mother's milk.
Porcupines enter
chewing bark and other things.

Lovers are not part of this design
but they wander through.
Hands holding, crushing asters.

Fall feels different,
color golden, translucent.
The quaking dispenses death,
touch of earth's decay.
Feeding ropes, they travel
new growth, new place.

A leaf from the Aspen.

Ginny Gaskill

In Stillness

A bench sits in stillness,
thousands of eyes watch.
Cranes, egrets, geese travel.
Sunflowers grow
eyes watch the progression.
Seedlings start
green, yellow, brown.
Tiny sparrows, finches feed.

Ginny Gaskill

Columbine

Columbine his favorite flower. Still cannot look at one
without longing, wanting. Remembering the softness in his
eyes as his fingers glide across petals. My garden filled
with thousands of blossoms but this species and daisies
make me stop and smile inside. They feed my longing.

Columbine minute
flowers formed, tall, yellow.
Seed pods, next years life.

Iris Gersh

Amaranth Haibun

He's popping the amaranth seeds on top of the wood stove.
If we eat two cups a day, he says we consume complete
protein with magnesium and calcium in quantity. If it's
good enough for the pre-Colombian Aztecs, it's good
enough for us, he says. Sure, can I load it with butter and
salt? I ask on day number three. No, no, defeats the
purpose. A warm nutty smell wafts into the room where our
cat jumps a foot each time he hears the tiny pops. After we
threw seeds into the dirt yard last fall, they grew and grew,
and dry muted-gold corn stalks now surround the once
purple-plumed plants. Corn, beans, squash, and the fourth
sister, amaranth.

> Sacred seeds sustain
> Fuchsia feathers spirit coat
> Amaranth power.

Jules Nyquist

Bosque Response

Sing to the plants
Don't you know they hear you?
Like two lovers communicate without words.
Stroke their leaves, water them gently.
Talk to them daily and they thrive.
Plant them next to each other so they can talk
the way they do.
Absorb each other's wisdom.
Add a few rocks.

The Bosque sings, if you listen.
Comforts with boughs of arms.
I have only one body here now to plant beauty,
begin to know what is contained in dirt.
A piece of sky lives here in the west mesa
connected to the world

Stop cutting down the trees.
Stop mining the mountains.
Stop plowing roads by the river.
Have you ever sat at a foot of a tree, to lean your back
against its cool bark, feel its life inside?
They are trying to tell us.

Jules Nyquist

Invocation

Who am I lead others
in poetry, a writing coach
when I am the one still learning?
Eyes open, ears ringing
reading other poets, their words mix with mine
books stacked, some signed
friends, mostly, our fellowship of words
process of observation.
Who am I to share the poet's path
except to say: come, here
take and eat
join the fellowship.
It is all good.

Susan Paquet

Difficult Migrations

The Cranes trumpet calls
my name as rolling sounds
traverse the clouds

I strain my neck to see
as only my eyes can climb
beyond my brown adobe wall
into the sea glass blue of sky

The Cranes travel
without elegance but with purpose
below their bodies
long legs are outstretched
immobile as are mine

Their flight is not the V pattern of geese
but a kaleidoscope of positions
desperately searching for safe landing
between housing developments, high rises
and asphalt of 2015

Their species refuses extinction
migrating with desire and determination

I myself, struggle to stand
awkwardly pushing my walker
determined to travel across my yard
for a better view of inspiration

Susan Paquet

Haiku

*In honor of Judith Roderick's beautiful tapestry
which hangs in the conference room of the Open
Space Visitor Center*

Tapestry of Cranes
threading replicates plumage
stitching wind to earth

Andi Penner

Eve, in the Bosque

A fat wasp burrows into a half-eaten apple.
The drying flesh lies exposed beneath leathery red skin.
Someone has been here before me.

From my wooden bench at the edge of the bosque,
I lift my face to the warm autumn sun
       and ponder cicada hum.

       Over my shoulder
       a *plein air* painter captures dying sunflowers
       and a cloudless sky
       from beneath her lavender hat.

She sees neither wasp nor apple—
as though we exist in parallel
universes,
each of us content
in her own bosque world.

The wasp burrows deeper
into the apple's flesh.
And I remember the sweet sting of your lips.

Karin Pitman

Mortality

Driving across the river, a few cottonwood leaves now
yellow hinting of fall caught my eye.
All of a sudden, soon, will come the tipping point of
more fall than winter, more yellow than green, more death
than life.

all yellow after
days of green long lazy done
quickly we will fall

Karin Pitman

Migrations, Transitions, Passages

Migrations, transitions, passages.
Earlier a major way of life.
By 14: Germany, Arkansas, Virginia, Arizona, Virginia
again, Arizona again, Gallup, Kansas, Panama.
Even in Panama: Clayton, Amador, then the City,
before back to Arizona and settling in Albuquerque.

Migrations, transitions, passages
are different now – vacations, job changes, finding and
losing friendships,
navigating the changes in life, in my body, in my world.
More settled and sedentary now, but still nothing constant.

Migrations, transitions, passages
will become more intellectual, emotional, spiritual
as years go by and my body winds down to resting
and stillness.

Karin Pitman

Edges

Edges, the play of contrasts: red plants against green
grasses
wild grasses against mowed lawn, trees as the termini.
But beyond are the grey purple Sandias, just before endless
blue sky into oblivion.
Manmade forms against one another: light and dark, soft
and textured.
My painter's eye feasts on the edges: places that create the
interest of a composition,
each requiring a decision: what brush,what paint, what
color, what richness or dullness?
Almost hard to turn if off just to enjoy the beauty of nature.

Karin Pitman

Hearth

Once a family gathered here, the ones who built me.
I was the center of love and laughter and music.

Then came a transition, letting go, loss of my family.
People discussing what to do with me, a time of
uncertainty, change.

Now I see life again, but less consistently.
There are days I spend alone, in quiet with the glory of
nature near.
Then people come to meet, to talk, to learn, to see and do.

Now I am surrounded by art and culture,
and still I give a presence and heart to what goes on here.

But I miss my family.

Scott Wiggerman

Open Space Corn

Narrowed to spines,
    the stalks stoop
        like penitents.

Brittle leaves
    the color of sand—
        and almost as coarse—

rasp in the breeze.
    Winter is not far off.
        And yet,

seedheads are pliant,
    as though hope
        fills their veins,

though individual
    grains no longer
        hug one another,

separate easily,
    sifting away
        like our lives.

Scott Wiggerman

Winterfat

This awful name
for something so gorgeous:
the soft mint-green
fluff of the spires,
like rabbit feet
begging to be petted;
leaves that peak
like crisp rows
of rosemary needles—
and below,
gangly, ragged,
stripped-down stems,
ready for winter,
apparently stored with fat.

Scott Wiggerman

Open Space Sunflowers

Taller than the tallest man,
rising into the bluest of blue

as if plant and sky
conspire in private.

Adobe walls, the bridge, myself—
clearly not needed.

Scott Wiggerman

Litany from the Tower

Follow . . . the sharp
outline of the Sandias
against the cloudless sky.

Follow . . . the still-green
line of cottonwoods
running below the mountains.

Follow . . . the vibrant
horizon of grass
beneath the trees.

Repeat . . .
Repeat . . .
Repeat . . .

Ruth Wilson

Look to What You Love

Wandering – I searched for self.
I looked to trees and sand and sky –
with their spirits
breathing light and loveliness.

And for my wondering soul –
was it whisperings or was it wishes? –
I don't really know,
but to find what I was searching for
the message was simple; the message was clear –
"Look to what you love; know what you hold dear.

Don't go to books; don't rely on words.
To discover who you are and what you might become,
sit awhile near a cottonwood tree,
bury your toes in the toasty sand,
disappear into the endless sky."

Photo Credits

Title		Taken by
Andi Penner & Susan Paquet at Open Space Visitor Center	vii	Jules Nyquist
Joanne Bodin by sculpture	1	Rona Fisher
Open Space Visitor Center	4	Jules Nyquist
Open Space Visitor Center	10	Jules Nyquist
Jules Nyquist leading work-shop at Open Space Visitor Center	13	Joanne Bodin
Backyard Patio at Jules' Nyquist's home	17	Jules Nyquist
Joanne Bodin at Open Space Visitor Center	19	Jules Nyquist
Open Space Garden	24	Jules Nyquist
Open Space Visitor Center	27	Jules Nyquist
Wall at Albuquerque Museum near Old Town	30	Jules Nyquist
Window at Open Space Visitor Center	32	Jules Nyquist

www.ingramcontent.com/pod-product-compliance
Lightning Source LLC
Chambersburg PA
CBHW050857290526
45792CB00002B/633